Who Is
Judy Blume?

by Kirsten Anderson

illustrated by Ted Hammond

Penguin Workshop
An Imprint of Penguin Random House

To Elaine, who taught me to read and shared Judy Blume books with me—KA

To my kids, Stephanie and Jason—TH

PENGUIN WORKSHOP
Penguin Young Readers Group
An Imprint of Penguin Random House LLC

Text copyright © 2018 by Kirsten Anderson. Illustrations copyright © 2018 by Penguin Random House LLC. All rights reserved. Published by Penguin Workshop, an imprint of Penguin Random House LLC, 345 Hudson Street, New York, New York 10014. PENGUIN and PENGUIN WORKSHOP are trademarks of Penguin Books Ltd. WHO HQ & Design is a registered trademark of Penguin Random House LLC. Printed in the USA.

Library of Congress Cataloging-in-Publication Data is available.

ISBN 9780448488493 (paperback)   10 9 8 7 6 5 4 3
ISBN 9781524788520 (library binding)   10 9 8 7 6 5 4 3 2 1

Contents

Who Is Judy Blume?

By 1968, Judy Blume had been writing stories and books for children for several years. She had sent her work to publishers but had only sold a few stories. That was a start, but she dreamed of having a book published.

Judy had been making up stories in her head her whole life, but she had only started to write them down when her children, Randy and Larry, began school. Without her kids at home, Judy didn't have much to do. She tried new hobbies. But she was bored. Then Judy tried writing. Suddenly, she had found something she loved to do. Writing was the easy part, though. The hard part was finding someone to publish what she wrote.

That changed when she got the phone call.

It was from a publishing company. They had read an idea for a picture book she had sent them called *The One in the Middle Is the Green Kangaroo*. And they wanted to publish it!

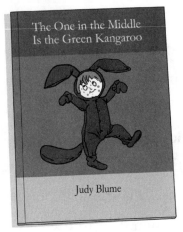

Judy was so excited. Someone actually was going to publish a book she had written! She ran down to the basement, where her children were playing with their friend Laurie. They were molding Silly Sand into different shapes. Judy grabbed handfuls of the Silly Sand and began to throw it into the air. She picked up her kids and spun them around. Laurie stared at Mrs.

Blume and then went home crying. Through her tears, she told her mother that Randy and Larry's mother had gone crazy.

Judy Blume hadn't gone crazy. She was simply celebrating. And—although she didn't know it— she was on her way to becoming one of the most popular children's authors of all time.

Every year, new generations of young readers discover her stories and see themselves in the characters she has created—kids who are just like them. They worry about the same embarrassing things. They struggle with the same problems. Through her characters, Judy has talked about many things other adults wouldn't explain.

And to her many fans, she has become a hero who lets them know that they aren't the only ones who question what is happening around them—with their families, their feelings, and even their own bodies. In Judy's books, young readers can see that the world isn't a perfect place, but it is often a hilarious one.

CHAPTER 1
Elizabeth, Miami, Elizabeth

Judith Sussman was born on February 12, 1938, in Elizabeth, New Jersey. Her father, Rudolph, was a dentist. Her mother, Esther, was a stay-at-home mom. She had a brother, David, who was four years older than her.

Her father was outgoing, fun loving, and adventurous. Her mother was quieter and worried about everything: She worried about her family getting hurt. She worried about whether Judy was doing well in school, about how Judy looked, and even if Judy had any friends. Judy was a combination of both her parents. She tried to be adventurous, but she also worried a lot.

Judy was very shy when she was young, but she always had a vivid imagination. She made up stories while she bounced a ball off the wall of the house. She took piano lessons, then pretended that she was a piano teacher with her own group of students. She even had a notebook in which she kept track of her imaginary students' lessons.

She dreamed of being a cowgirl, a spy, an actress, a ballerina, or a detective when she grew up.

Judy's father was an air-raid warden during World War II. He was supposed to help move people to safer places if the town of Elizabeth were ever bombed. Her mother and grandmother knitted sweaters to send to the soldiers fighting in Europe. The whole family sat around the radio in the evenings and listened to news about the war.

Judy could hear her parents whispering about it late at night. She worried about the possibility of the war coming to America and about her town being bombed.

Her stories were her escape, though. In real life, she might have feared many things. But in the stories she made up, Judy always beat the enemy. She was always brave and strong. She was the hero.

Although this made her feel better, she kept her stories secret. Adults often seemed to have secrets. Why shouldn't she have them, too?

Judy loved going to the movies and reading. She would visit the library and just wander past the shelves, picking up anything that looked interesting. Her favorite books were the Nancy Drew series, the Oz books, and the Betsy-Tacy books, about two friends in Minnesota.

The Betsy-Tacy Books

The Betsy-Tacy books are a series of thirteen books written by Maud Hart Lovelace. Based on Lovelace's memories of her own childhood, the books describe the adventures of Betsy and Tacy, two friends growing up in Minnesota in the early years of the twentieth century.

The first book begins when Betsy and Tacy meet at age five; the last one ends in 1917, when Betsy is married and her husband is getting ready to go off to fight in World War I.

The books were published from 1940 to 1955. Young girls who began reading the series in the early '40s grew up with the stories of Betsy and Tacy.

The series still has many fans today, as one generation of readers has passed the books down to another.

In 1946, Judy's brother became very sick. His doctor suggested that moving to a warmer place might help David's health. Judy and her mother, brother, and grandmother all moved to Miami, Florida, for the year. Her father stayed in New Jersey to be near his patients and continue working. He came to visit the rest of the family in Florida once a month.

At first Judy hated being away from home. She was only nine years old. And she worried about how her father was doing all alone back in New Jersey. But then she started to have fun. She went roller-skating and rode her bike. She visited the nearby beach and swam in the Atlantic Ocean. She took ballet lessons. And she made new friends.

Judy began to change while she was in Florida. She became more outgoing. When she returned home to New Jersey, she was no longer shy. She began to spend more time with her friends and at school activities. In seventh grade, she became best friends with a girl named Mary Sullivan. They were inseparable.

Judy's brother was quiet and didn't work very hard in school. Judy often felt she had to work twice as hard to make up for David. She put a lot of effort into her studies and tried to please her parents. She kept all her worries to herself and always acted happy. But sometimes the stress was too much for Judy. Throughout her childhood, she was sick with stomach trouble and skin problems.

When Judy got to middle school, she found that books written for girls that age didn't interest her. She didn't care for stories about girls with horses or girls who grew up on farms out on the prairie. She wanted to read books about a girl like her, with some of her same problems. Sometimes she even made up books for her school book reports! Some were about the adventures of a horse named Dobbin, because she thought that sounded like the type of book teachers would expect her to read. She often got As on her fake reports because they sounded so much like real books!

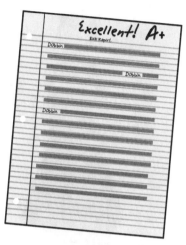

None of the books Judy was *supposed* to like answered the kinds of questions that were on her mind. She and her friends wanted to know more about what it was like to be grown-up and to learn all the details they could about their changing bodies. But the adults they knew either avoided their questions or gave them scientific explanations that didn't help much.

Judy and her friends promised that they would share all their experiences and tell one another how they really felt. That's what friends were for.

But still, Judy had thoughts and feelings she didn't understand. She didn't want scientific explanations; she wanted to know what puberty

would *really* be like. She wondered if she was the only one who felt this way. Was she normal? Judy wished there was a book that told her that she wasn't alone with her thoughts and emotions. But there wasn't.

CHAPTER 2
Mrs. Blume

Beginning in 1952, Judy went to an all-girls high school. She kept busy with many activities. She joined a school dance group and sang in the chorus. She and Mary Sullivan were coeditors of the school newspaper. They tried out for plays and dreamed about becoming famous actresses. They had a lot of fun together.

Judy graduated from high school in 1956 and was accepted at Boston University. She planned to study education so she could become a teacher. But she knew that she would also be looking for a husband. In the 1950s,  most young women were encouraged to get married and have children as soon as they could. They didn't always plan to have careers. Many women who did work quit their jobs as soon as they got married. Attending college was one way to meet young men who would soon have good jobs.

Just before she left for Boston, Judy began to feel sick. She was very tired all the time. Within two weeks of starting college, she couldn't even go to classes.

Finally, she went to a doctor and was told she had mononucleosis (say: mon-oh-noo-klee-OH-sis), which is sometimes just called "mono." Judy was sent back home to New Jersey.

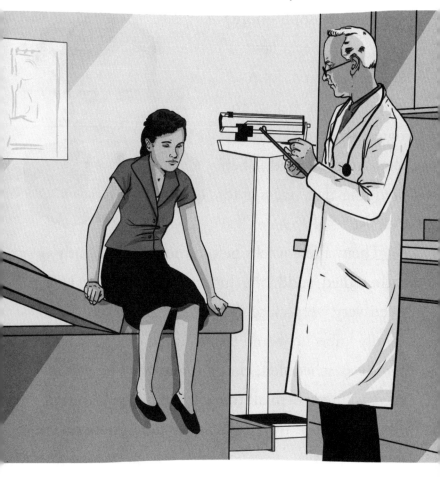

It took months for Judy to fully recover. She decided not to go back to Boston. Instead, she enrolled at New York University (NYU), which is in New York City and was much closer to home.

During her sophomore year, Judy met a law student named John Blume. They began to date. After ten months, they were engaged. Their wedding day was set for August 15, 1959.

Then, a few weeks before the wedding, Judy's father died suddenly. Judy and her father had been very, very close. She was heartbroken. The family knew he would have wanted everything to go on as scheduled, though, and that he would have wanted them all to have a good time. But it was hard for Judy to have happy memories of her wedding day.

Judy graduated from NYU in 1961 with a degree in education. That same year, her daughter, Randy, was born. Her son, Lawrence, known as Larry, was born two years later in 1963.

The Blumes settled into a home in Scotch Plains, New Jersey. Judy didn't have much in common with the other young mothers in town.

She tried to do the same things they did. She took golf and tennis lessons, but she didn't really enjoy them. She went shopping, but that bored her. She didn't have any close friends in her neighborhood.

Mary had also gotten married, but she lived in New York City, and the two friends rarely got together. Judy felt lonely. She often felt sick, just like she had as a child. She thought it was because she wasn't happy.

Judy seemed to have everything: a husband and two wonderful children who she loved very much, and a beautiful house in a nice town. But she wanted something more.

CHAPTER 3
Mom Writes Books for Little Children

In the late 1960s, when both Randy and Larry had started school, Judy had a lot more free time. She noticed the world changing around her. African Americans and American women were fighting for their rights and equality. Rock music, movies, and art were all encouraging people to do what made them happy instead of what others expected them to do.

Judy felt frustrated. She wanted to *do* something! She had been very creative as a child but had not used that creativity in a long time. She tried writing songs. She tried making and selling felt banners. And she wondered what else she could try. Why not write stories? This was Judy's best idea yet.

All her life, Judy had made up stories. She told her children stories, and she invented stories for herself while she washed dishes or did other housework. It had never occurred to her that she could actually be a writer. It was time to try.

Judy began to write stories for children. She remembered her own childhood in great detail, so it made sense to write about her youth. She wrote picture books and drew the pictures herself, though she didn't think she was a very good artist.

Early responses to her work were not very encouraging. Publishers rejected her story and book ideas. She showed her work to one of John's friends who had studied literature in college. He told her that she couldn't write. One publisher sent back one of her picture books with a note that said she had no talent and should just give up.

But Judy didn't give up. Instead, she just kept writing. She studied books by popular children's authors such as Beverly Cleary, Louise Fitzhugh, and E. L. Konigsburg and tried to learn from them. She still couldn't get any publishers interested in her work, though.

Then one day she received a notice in the mail. New York University was offering a class on how

to write for children. It was perfect timing. The class seemed to be exactly what Judy needed.

And it was. Each week at home, Judy wrote pages and pages of new stories. Then, one night a week, she took the train into New York City for her class. Her professor saw that Judy had a talent for writing about real kids and very real situations and told her to stick with it.

Beverly Cleary (1916–)

As a young girl in Oregon, Beverly Cleary struggled to learn to read. But a kind school librarian found books to help her improve, and eventually Beverly fell in love with reading.

Beverly herself grew up to become a school librarian. When she had a hard time finding books that would appeal to kids who had difficulty reading, she decided to start writing her own. In 1950, her first novel, *Henry Huggins*, was published. She followed that with a series of books about kids who lived in Henry's neighborhood, including her most famous character, Ramona Quimby. Her stories were based on characters and events she remembered from her childhood.

Beverly Cleary has written more than forty books that have sold over ninety-one million copies. She has won many awards and influenced other children's book authors, including Judy Blume.

Judy took the class twice. She was working on a novel called *Iggie's House*. In 1968, the US government passed the Fair Housing Act. It meant that people could not be stopped from buying or renting a home in a certain neighborhood just because of their race, religion, gender, or nationality. For the first time, people of color were able to move into previously all-white areas. In Judy's book, a young white girl befriends the first African American family to move into her neighborhood.

One day Judy saw an ad in a magazine. A new publisher called Bradbury Press was looking for authors of children's fiction about real-life kids. This was exactly what Judy was writing about! She sent the manuscript of *Iggie's House* to the company.

Dick Jackson and Bob Verrone, the editors at Bradbury, liked it very much. They especially thought the characters' conversations sounded real. Judy met with Dick Jackson. He suggested some changes to make *Iggie's House* better. Judy made the changes, and he agreed to publish it.

She also had just gotten the news that *The One in the Middle Is the Green Kangaroo* would be published by Reilly & Lee Books. Judy was finally beginning to feel like a real author!

Some people didn't take Judy's success seriously, though. After *Green Kangaroo* was published, a local newspaper wrote an article titled "Mom Keeps Busy Writing Books for Little Children."

Her husband joked that writing was a better hobby than shopping and spending money. Everyone thought writing was just something Judy did to pass the time. But it had become her true passion.

CHAPTER 4
Enter Margaret

Judy was anxious to write another book. She thought about how frustrated she had been by some of the stories she had read when she was eleven or twelve years old. She had looked for books about a girl who had the same questions and concerns that she had at that age. She had never found them. Now she decided to write the kind of book she had always wanted to read.

Judy wrote about many of the experiences and feelings that she had had when she was twelve. She didn't think about what other children's books were like and what those books weren't supposed to talk about. Instead, she said, "For the first time since I'd started writing, I let go and this story came pouring out. I felt as if I'd always known Margaret."

The book is about Margaret Simon, an *almost* twelve-year-old girl whose family has just moved from New York City to a town in New Jersey. Margaret has to go to a new school and make new friends. At the same time, she is struggling with questions about religion. She wonders about her changing body as she begins puberty. Margaret worries about fitting in with her new friends and whether she is "normal," like other girls. She worries about her feelings and what they mean. She is a sixth-grader who talks to God about her faith, her family, boys, bras, and getting her period.

To Get
☐ A Date
☐ A Bra
☐ My Period

These were all the questions and worries Judy had experienced when she was growing up! But no one had ever discussed them. Most of these subjects were things that people just didn't talk about with children. They thought that subjects like puberty were taboo. But Judy thought they were important. She said, "I wanted to be honest. And I felt that no adult had been honest with me. We didn't have the information we should have had."

The book was published in 1970. Margaret was a new kind of character for young readers. She wondered about all sorts of things, like when to start

using deodorant. "I don't use deodorant yet. I don't think people start to smell bad until they're at least twelve. So I've still got a few months to go." This was a very different sort of story!

What Are Taboos?

Taboos are things that are considered too impolite to talk about or that are simply forbidden.

Before the 1970s, children's books avoided many taboos. Very few authors felt free to write about certain taboo topics, including:

- Kids questioning their changing bodies, emotions, and sexuality during puberty
- Drug use
- Alcohol use
- Girls getting their periods
- Physical disabilities

When Judy Blume wrote about these sorts of things, she said, "I wanted to tell the truth as I knew it." She was not afraid of the taboos.

The *New York Times* reviewed *Are You There, God? It's Me, Margaret*, praising it as "funny, warm and loving." The paper also named it one of their "Outstanding Books of the Year"! When Judy's editor read her the review over the phone, Judy was so stunned that she fell to her knees. She couldn't believe that something she had written had gotten such a positive review in an important newspaper.

Are You There, God? It's Me, Margaret became more and more popular. Publishers had recently begun to put out pocket-size paperbacks of their books. The paperbacks were inexpensive, usually less than a dollar, which meant that even kids could afford to buy their own copies of *Margaret*. More and more girls discovered it, and Judy began to get fan mail from them. They told her they felt just like Margaret. They thought of Margaret as a friend. They felt that way about Judy, too.

For her next book, Judy thought it would be interesting to write about a boy and the challenges he was facing. *Then Again, Maybe I Won't* is about Tony Miglione, a twelve-year-old boy. Like Margaret's, Tony's life is changing. His family has suddenly become rich, and they move to a wealthy suburb where they struggle to fit in. Like Margaret, Tony also worries about his body and his emotions. Making the move from little kid to teenager is *not* easy!

Then Again, Maybe I Won't was published in 1971. It also got good reviews. Now it was clear that writing was not just a hobby. Judy had become a successful author.

CHAPTER 5
Fudge and Other Tales

Judy began to write as fast as she could. In 1972, she published three books!

One was called *It's Not the End of the World*. It is about a girl who is struggling with her parents' divorce.

In the early 1970s, divorce was becoming more common, but it could still seem unusual in a lot of places. Many children of divorce might not have known anyone else who had divorced parents. And maybe they sometimes felt alone and unsure of the world. Judy's main character, Karen, had the same fears and doubts that many of her young readers did.

After her success with *Are You There God? It's Me, Margaret*, Judy expanded on a short story she had written years earlier about a toddler who  had swallowed a turtle. The story turned into a book about a nine-year-old boy named Peter Hatcher, and his brother, two-and-a-half-year-old Farley Drexel Hatcher, who insists on being called Fudge. Fudge is always getting into some kind of trouble. He annoys and embarrasses Peter, who thinks Fudge is allowed to get away with too much.

Judy based Fudge on her son, Larry, and how he had behaved when he was a toddler. Many of Fudge's stunts were things that Larry had done—except he never swallowed a turtle.

She wrote the book quickly. Judy showed it to her editor, who thought it was just perfect.

She wanted to publish it right away. Judy was used to making changes and rewriting her books—or parts of them—several times. This was the only one that she "got right" on the first try.

How Embarrassing Could Fudge Be?

In *Tales of a Fourth Grade Nothing*, Peter's little brother, Fudge, seems to constantly top himself in the embarrassing department. Throughout the course of the series, Fudge actually:

- Eats flowers
- Refuses to eat unless he is fed like a dog

- Swallows Peter's turtle
- Hides his baby sister in a closet
- Tries to sell his baby sister
- Calls his kindergarten teacher "Rat Face"

Peter may have hated Fudge's antics, but readers loved them. *Tales of a Fourth Grade Nothing* became one of Judy's most popular books.

Judy's next book was called *Otherwise Known as Sheila the Great*. It features a character from *Tales of a Fourth Grade Nothing*, Peter's neighbor and sworn enemy. But although Sheila Tubman acts brave and tough, inside she is deeply afraid of many things: thunderstorms, the dark, dogs, and swimming. Those were all things Judy had feared when she was a young girl, too. *Otherwise Known as Sheila the Great* tells the story of the summer when Sheila Tubman overcomes many of her fears.

Judy continued to find inspiration for books all around her. She met a girl who needed to wear a back brace to correct her crooked spine. That led to Judy's book *Deenie*. Her next book, called *The Pain and the Great One*, is about a sister and brother who don't get along. It was directly inspired by her daughter, Randy, and son, Larry, and how they competed with each other when they were very young. They even called each other "The Pain" and "The Great One"!

Randy was in middle school when she told her mother how some kids in her class had decided to pick on one girl. That gave Judy the idea for *Blubber*, a story about bullying and how it can happen to anyone.

When Randy became a teenager, she told her mom that most of the books she read about teens in love seemed to always end with bad things happening to them. She said she wished she could find a book about two kids who are in love who didn't have their romance turn into some kind of disaster.

Judy wrote *Forever*, the story of Katherine and Michael, two average high-school students and how they meet and fall in love. Nothing terrible happens, and they aren't punished for their relationship.

Believe it or not, this was very unusual in the 1970s!

Judy was dealing with her own real-life breakup. She and John had been married for sixteen years. They had gotten married when they were very young. Judy had become a very different person. She had grown and changed. And she wanted to try new things. She and John divorced in 1975.

The divorce was very hard on the Blume family. Judy had written about how families deal with divorce in *It's Not the End of the World*. But that didn't make it any easier in real life.

CHAPTER 6
New Mexico

Judy was single for the first time in her adult life—but not for long. She started dating a scientist named Thomas Kitchens, and they married only a few months later in 1976. She knew almost right away that they had made a mistake. They had barely known each other.

Thomas's job was suddenly moved to New Mexico. So Judy and her two children packed up and left New Jersey. She was very unhappy in New Mexico, but she kept writing. She said, "I've always been able to write, even when everything else was falling apart."

Judy's next book, *Starring Sally J. Freedman as Herself*, was about a very different time and place. It was set in Miami during the 1940s and was directly based on Judy's own experiences when she had moved there with her brother, mother, and grandmother. Many of the things that happened to Sally were also things that had happened to Judy. And like Judy, Sally was a very imaginative girl who was always making up stories.

After *Sally*, Judy wrote a book that was also about her own life. But it was very different. It was written for adults.

People were shocked when Judy's novel *Wifey* was published in 1978. They couldn't believe that a successful children's author like Judy Blume would suddenly write a book for adults. Some of her fans even worried that she was going to completely stop writing for children.

But Judy was just doing what she often did: writing about what she saw around her. *Wifey* was about a woman who was unhappy with her marriage. And that's how Judy felt, too. She divorced Thomas Kitchens in 1979 but decided to stay in New Mexico so Larry could finish school. Randy had already left for college.

Kids had been begging Judy to write another book about Fudge and Peter Hatcher since *Tales of a Fourth Grade Nothing* had been published in 1972. One day, she suddenly thought of an idea for a book: What if Peter and Fudge had a baby sister or brother? Judy knew that Peter would worry that he would have to deal with another embarrassing troublemaker like Fudge. And Fudge would get into even more trouble, working hard to make sure he got enough attention.

Superfudge was published in 1980. And Judy's fans loved it. In 1982, the American Library Association ran a poll to find out the fifty most-popular children's books in the country. Thousands of children responded, and they voted *Superfudge* number one.

Judy decided she wanted to do more for her readers and for all kids. In 1981, she created *The Judy Blume Diary*, a one-year journal that encouraged children to write about themselves and their feelings. She used the profits from the diary to establish the Kids Fund. The fund donated money to different children's organizations. Some worked with teen mothers, while others helped kids deal with their parents' divorces.

Larry graduated from high school, and Judy began to think about leaving New Mexico. She had always wanted to live in New York City. So in 1981, she moved there. Judy enjoyed walking around the streets and hearing people's conversations. She also began to take tap-dancing classes. She had always loved dancing and was excited to return to it. She worked very hard and enjoyed being in classes with people who were professional dancers and actors in Broadway shows.

Judy started work on a new book. She thought she would write the story and characters the way she wanted, and the book would be published as usual. But she was wrong. The world was changing. And some people had started paying close attention to the taboo subjects in Judy's books.

CHAPTER 7
Banned Books

Judy's next book was called *Tiger Eyes*. It was about Davey, a girl whose father is killed during a robbery. Davey, her mother, and her younger brother go to New Mexico to try to recover from the tragedy. Slowly, Davey begins to heal and to feel love again.

When Judy met with her editor in New York, he was concerned about the section of the book where Davey talked honestly about her body and feelings. Judy had written about fifteen-year-old girls and their daydreams and crushes on boys in many of her other books. No one had questioned it. That was part of Judy's famous honesty that kids loved.

Her editor explained that now some parents

were beginning to protest that kind of honesty. They felt their children shouldn't be reading so many details about bodies, emotions, and growing up. Judy's editor didn't want to upset parents who might tell school libraries to take the book off their shelves or not buy it at all.

Judy hesitated. The details of Davey's story made sense to her. She didn't want to change it. But she didn't want her book kept out of school libraries, either. Judy reluctantly agreed. But she decided that she would never again give in to pressure to change the things she believed in.

The 1970s had been a very open time. People felt free to do, say, and try new things.

The 1980s were very different, though. The world was becoming more cautious. Parents began to worry about what music their kids were listening to and what books they were reading. Some told schools that they thought Judy's books should be banned, or kept out of their school libraries. They complained to school boards and town governments. Some schools agreed and removed Judy's books. Others said that only older students or those with permission from their parents could read them.

A college professor did a study of which authors were most banned in schools from 1970 to 1984. He found that Judy Blume was one of the most banned authors in the United States.

People challenged Judy's books for many different reasons. They wanted *Are You There, God? It's Me, Margaret*; *Then Again, Maybe I Won't*; *Deenie*; and *Forever* banned because of their honesty about kids' changing bodies during puberty. Some parents didn't even like the idea of their daughters reading about getting their periods!

Other parents complained about a few curse words in *It's Not the End of the World*. They felt that *Blubber* was dangerous because the bullies in the classroom are not punished. Some groups just wanted *all* of Judy's books banned from their schools!

Judy was shocked. She didn't think there was anything wrong with her books. She knew that kids liked them. They wrote to her all the time, thanking her for creating such realistic characters. She didn't believe in censorship—when people exclude things that are considered offensive— or banning books because of taboos. Judy was very frustrated. She later said, "This is America: We don't have censorship, we have, you know, freedom to read, freedom to write, freedom of the press, we don't do this, we don't ban books. But then they did."

Judy began to speak out. Other authors of banned books supported her as well. In 1982, the American Library Association (ALA) began to hold Banned Books Week every year to make people aware of the dangers of censorship. They published lists of the most frequently challenged, protested, and banned books and authors. The ALA felt that readers should make up their own minds.

They did not wantto be told to pull certain books from library shelves.

Judy became active with an organization called the National Coalition Against Censorship (NCAC). The NCAC works directly with authors whose books are in danger of being banned. They help librarians or teachers who have lost their jobs for protecting banned books. They support legal cases to have court decisions overturned, so that banned books will be allowed in classrooms and libraries.

Some parents joined the fight as well. They thought that their children should have the freedom to choose what they read. These parents sued school districts—and sometimes their own

towns—to get the banned books put back in their libraries. Kids helped by writing letters or speaking at meetings, saying that they wanted their favorite authors and books back.

Judy passionately believed that openness and honesty were good for kids and that hiding information from them was bad. She worried about young readers who wouldn't have the right books to help them with their questions about life. She feared that some authors would now be too careful because they were afraid of being banned.

Judy said, "But it's not just the books under fire now that worry me. It is the books that will never be written. . . . As always, young readers will be the real losers."

Judy Blume Gets Challenged!

According to the American Library Association, Judy Blume is one of the most frequently challenged authors of the twenty-first century. *Challenged* means that someone has asked for a book to be removed from a school or a library's shelves. If the town or school board agrees, the book is banned from that school or library.

Judy Blume has had:

• Two books on the Frequently Challenged Children's Books list: *Are You There, God? It's Me, Margaret* and *Blubber*

• Four books on the Frequently Challenged Young Adult Books list: *Deenie*; *Forever*; *Here's to You, Rachel Robinson*; and *Tiger Eyes*

• Five books on the 100 Most Frequently Challenged Books: 1990–1999 list: *Forever*; *Blubber*; *Deenie*; *Are You There, God? It's Me, Margaret*; and *Tiger Eyes*

CHAPTER 8
Letters to Judy

Judy did not let any "banned books" lists keep her from writing. In 1983, she wrote a book for adults called *Smart Women*. Although the main characters were two grown women, their teenage daughters were also major characters in the book. Judy thought the daughters were two of her best teenage characters yet.

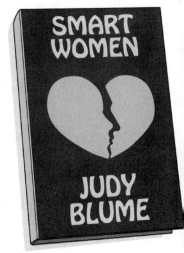

She continued to get thousands of letters from her fans. Some wrote to say how much they liked her books. But others asked Judy for advice! Some told her their deepest secrets and worries.

They told her things they were too embarrassed to tell their parents or even their friends.

Judy tried to answer as many as possible. She wondered why kids would tell such important things to someone they had never met. She thought maybe her readers felt she understood them because her characters seemed so much like real kids. And maybe because, as Judy said, it was easier to tell secrets to someone "you don't have to face at the breakfast table the next morning."

She wished that parents could see the letters so they could understand their children better.

That wish turned into *Letters to Judy: What Your Kids Wish They Could Tell You.* Published in 1986, the book was filled with real letters Judy had received from young readers and her answers to them. All the money she made from the book went to her Kids Fund foundation. She hoped that parents who read the book would begin to listen more carefully to their children.

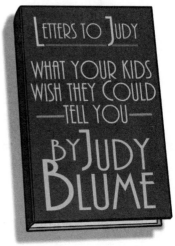

In 1987, Judy published *Just as Long as We're Together.* She had been thinking about the book's three main characters for years, but hadn't been able to find a way to put them into a story together. But finally she sat down and wrote about Stephanie, Rachel, and Alison, who find their friendships—and their whole world—changing as they enter seventh grade. The story is told by Stephanie, whose life gets even more complicated when her parents decide to get divorced. Judy began to write the book on a visit to Westport,

Connecticut. She liked the town and based most of the settings in the book on places she visited there. Alison's dog was even based on a dog Judy met in a Westport furniture store!

Judy's personal life also was finally settled. Her daughter, Randy, had become an airline pilot. Larry was working in the movie business. And in 1987, Judy and George Cooper, a law professor she had met in Santa Fe, got married.

Larry wanted to make movies based on his mother's books. Up until this time, *Forever* was the only book that had been made into a TV movie. None of Judy's other books had been filmed. Larry and Judy decided to turn *Otherwise Known as Sheila the Great* into a TV movie. Judy wrote the screenplay, and Larry directed it. Judy had a lot of fun making the movie and was very happy with how it turned out.

Judy hadn't planned to write another book about Fudge and Peter. But when she and George went on vacation to Maine, Judy saw a rope swing hanging from a tree in the yard next to their house. She pictured Sheila swinging on it.

Suddenly she had an idea for a whole new book about Fudge, Peter, and Sheila in Maine. That book became *Fudge-a-Mania*. It was published in 1990 and was very popular, just like the other Fudge books.

Next, Judy wanted to get back to writing more about the girls in *Just as Long as We're Together*. She spent time working on a possible TV series about them, but that didn't work out. When she finally had time to write, Judy decided to tell the story from Rachel's point of view. In *Here's to You, Rachel Robinson*, Rachel is a very intelligent girl who wants everything to be perfect. She takes classes above her grade level, and her teachers expect a lot from her. But that just makes her feel different and awkward with other kids her age, including her best friends. To make matters worse, her troublemaking brother,

Charles, is expelled from his boarding school. He comes home and makes Rachel's life miserable.

Judy got part of the idea for Rachel's character from a girl she knew in school who wanted everything to be perfect. Rachel also was inspired by a twelve-year-old girl who took college-level courses instead of regular classes in school.

She had written a letter to Judy saying that she felt out of place and lonely. Rachel was a very unusual character for Judy, but she knew that she had readers out there who would identify with her.

CHAPTER 9
Starring Judy Blume as Herself

In 1995, *Tales of a Fourth Grade Nothing* and *Superfudge* were used as the inspiration for a movie simply called *Fudge*. A Fudge TV show followed, just a year later. Fans were thrilled to see Peter, Fudge, and Sheila in their own TV show.

Judy and George bought a house on Martha's Vineyard, an island off the coast of Massachusetts. They split their time between Martha's Vineyard, New York City, and Key West, Florida.

Over the years, Judy and Mary Sullivan (now Mary Weaver), her best friend from middle school, had stayed in touch. Now she and Judy live near each other again, just like when they were young girls.

Summer Sisters, Judy's next book, was about two girls who form a lifelong friendship in middle school. That was like Mary and Judy's friendship, although Judy said that the characters had different experiences than they had had. *Summer Sisters* was written for adults. By this time, many of the adults who read it were women who had grown up reading Judy's books for children.

It had taken Judy years to write *Summer Sisters*. It was finally published in 1998. Readers loved it, and the book became a best seller. Judy said she wasn't interested in writing another novel for adults.

But she had once said she would never write about Fudge again, either. But then she had a grandson named Elliot. He loved to hear Fudge stories and begged Judy to write another.

In *Double Fudge*, Fudge spends his time trying to come up with new schemes to earn money. But his real problem is a three-year-old cousin named Farley Drexel—just like him! The new Farley also gets into a lot of trouble—just like him. Readers were, of course, happy to see Fudge again.

Judy continued her fight against book censorship. And in 1999, she wrote about the

movement by many schools to ban the Harry Potter books. Judy noted that her books had been targeted by angry parents for being too realistic in many ways. Now, the Harry Potter books were being challenged because they were fantasy. Judy wondered why parents didn't understand that interesting books encourage kids to read—and that was a *good* thing!

In 2002, a school board and group of parents won a court case that allowed them to ban the Harry Potter books from their school libraries. Judy and other authors joined the fight to have that decision overturned. The judge agreed, and the books were returned to the libraries.

In 2009, Judy heard another author talking about her latest book. It was a story that was set in the 1950s. That made Judy think about her own life during that time. She had never believed anything interesting enough for a good story had happened then! But suddenly she had an idea. Her book *In the Unlikely Event* was published in 2015. The story is about the town of Elizabeth, New Jersey, where Judy herself had grown up in the 1950s. As always, her characters are searching for happiness, and Judy's message is to never let fear limit your possibilities.

Judy still takes tap-dancing classes when she can and starts her day with a long walk. She tries to write every day when she's working on a book. And she and George are cofounders of a nonprofit bookstore in Key West, Florida, called Books & Books.

Words of Wisdom from Judy Blume

• If you don't have dreams, what do you have?

• Having the freedom to read and the freedom to choose is one of the best gifts my parents ever gave me.

• Librarians save lives: by handing the right book, at the right time, to a kid in need.

• We can have our beliefs and still read and discuss things.

• My only advice is to stay aware, listen carefully, and yell for help if you need it.

The store opened in 2016. Judy says, "I laugh now at how little we knew about running a bookstore." She spends much of her time there.

Instead of letters, Judy now gets e-mails from her many fans. Some are lifelong fans who grew up with her books. Others are new readers who are just discovering them. She tries to write back to as many as she can.

Judy Blume grew up in a time when adults seemed to keep many secrets from kids. When she started writing, most children's books avoided

certain issues, like puberty and the confusing emotions that come with it. But that all changed with *Are You There, God? It's Me, Margaret* and Judy's other books. Suddenly authors felt free to write about kids the way they really are. Books for young readers became much more realistic—and more helpful.

In time, Judy's contributions to children's literature were recognized. In 1996, she was given the Margaret A. Edwards Award from the American Library Association. She was named a Living Legend by the Library of Congress in 2000.

And she received the Distinguished Contribution to American Letters Medal of the National Book Foundation in 2004.

Judy didn't set out to break the rules. She just remembered very clearly how she had felt when she was young. She expressed her worries and doubts through the characters she created. Her books appealed to young people because the feelings, confusion, and concerns she wrote about were very real. It turns out that they weren't just her feelings. Her fans felt the same way, too.

Many people have grown up reading Judy Blume's books. She has sold over eighty-six million of them!

Judy often meets some of her readers who now have children of their own at book events or in restaurants or stores. It's very common for them to cry when they meet her. She thinks she knows why: "It's because I'm their childhood. . . . I remind them of their childhood."

Timeline of Judy Blume's Life

1938 — Born Judith Sussman on February 12 in Elizabeth, New Jersey

1959 — Marries John Blume

1961 — Daughter, Randy, is born

— Graduates from New York University

1963 — Son, Lawrence, is born

1969 — First book, *The One in the Middle Is the Green Kangaroo*, is published

1970 — *Iggie's House* and *Are You There, God? It's Me, Margaret* are published

1972 — *It's Not the End of the World*, *Tales of a Fourth Grade Nothing*, and *Otherwise Known as Sheila the Great* are published

1975 — Divorces John Blume

1976 — Marries Thomas Kitchens

1978 — *Wifey*, her first novel for adults, is published

1979 — Divorces Thomas Kitchens

1980 — *Superfudge* is published

1987 — Marries George Cooper

1996 — Receives Margaret A. Edwards Award from the ALA

2000 — Named a Living Legend by the Library of Congress

2018 — Receives the Carl Sandburg Literary Award from the Chicago Public Library

Timeline of the World

1939 — World War II begins in Europe

1940 — Color television is invented

1945 — World War II ends

1957 — The Soviet Union launches Sputnik, the world's first satellite, into space

1961 — LEGO building blocks are introduced in the United States

1962 — Andy Warhol's soup-can paintings are first shown in a Los Angeles art gallery

1969 — Hundreds of thousands of people come to upstate New York to take part in the Woodstock rock music festival

1974 — President Richard Nixon is forced to resign after the Watergate scandal

1977 — Steve Jobs, Steve Wozniak, and Ronald Wayne start Apple Computer

1985 — The first Super Mario Bros. game is released in North America

1995 — *Toy Story*, the first full-length computer-animated movie, is released

1997 — The Pathfinder spacecraft lands on Mars

2004 — Facebook is founded

2016 — Michael Phelps sets record for most Olympic medals after winning his twenty-eighth at the Rio Summer Olympics

Bibliography

*Books for young readers

Alter, Alexandra, and Kathryn Shattuck. "What Judy Blume's Books Meant." *New York Times*, June 1, 2015.

*Blume, Judy, and Lena Dunham. *Judy Blume and Lena Dunham in Conversation.* San Francisco, CA: Believer Books, 2013.

Broderick, Dorothy. "The Young Teen Scene." *New York Times*, November 8, 1970.

Dominus, Susan. "Judy Blume Knows All Your Secrets." *New York Times Magazine*, May, 18, 2015.

Flood, Alison. "Judy Blume: 'I thought, this is America: we don't ban books. But then we did.'" *The Guardian*, July 11, 2014.

Green, Michelle. "After Two Divorces, Judy Blume Blossoms as An Unmarried Woman—and Hits the Best-Seller List Again." *People*, March 19, 1984.

Oppenheimer, Mark. "Why Judy Blume Endures." *New York Times*, November 16, 1997.

Richards, Linda. "Judy Blume: On Censorship, Enjoying Life, and Staying in the Spotlight for Twenty-Five Years." *January Magazine*, 1998.

*Tracy, Kathleen. *Judy Blume: A Biography*. Westport, CT: Greenwood Press, 2008.

*Weidt, Maryann N. *Presenting Judy Blume*. Boston: Twayne Publishers, 1990.

Whitworth, Melissa. "Judy Blume's Lessons in Love." *The Telegraph*, February 3, 2008.